UNDERSTANDING ROMAN MYTHS

ROBIN JOHNSON

Crabtree Publishing Company

www.crabtreebooks.com

Author: Robin Johnson
Publishing plan research and development:
 Sean Charlebois, Reagan Miller
 Crabtree Publishing Company
Editor-in-chief: Lionel Bender
Editors: Simon Adams, Lynn Peppas
Proofreaders: Laura Booth, Wendy Scavuzzo
Project coordinator: Kathy Middleton
Photo research: Kim Richardson
Designer: Ben White
Cover design: Margaret Amy Salter
Production coordinator and Prepress technician:
 Margaret Amy Salter
Production: Kim Richardson
Print coordinator: Katherine Berti

Consultants: Noreen Doyle, M.A. Egyptology, M.A.
Nautical Archaeology, B.A. Anthropology, Art, and
Classical Civilizations: Author and consultant, Maine;
and Amy Leggett-Caldera, M.Ed., Elementary and
Middle School Education Consultant, Mississippi
State University.

Cover: Colosseum in Rome, Italy (top center); Portrait
of Hadrian as the god Mars (top left); Statue of a male
deity known as "Jupiter of Smyrna" (top right); Roman
mosaic (bottom)

Title page: A statue of Hercules outside the
Hoffberg Palace

Photographs and reproductions:
Maps: Stefan Chabluk
Front cover: Wikimedia Commons: Jastrow: top left and right;
Shutterstock: top center; Wikimedia Commons: Joanbanjo: bottom
The Art Archive: 10–11 (Archaeological Museum Milan/Collection
Dagli Orti), 14 (Museo Prenestino Palestrina/Collection Dagli Orti), 16
(Museo della Civilta Romana Rome/Gianni Dagli Orti), 17
(Archaeological Museum Palermo/Gianni Dagli Orti), 19
(Archaeological Museum Cherchel Algeria/Gianni Dagli Orti), 24
(Museo della Civilta Romana Rome/Gianni Dagli Orti), 27t (Gianni
Dagli Orti), 29 (Museo della Civilta Romana Rome/Gianni Dagli Orti),
32 (Museo Palazzo dei Conservatori Rome/Gianni Dagli Orti), 33t
(Musée du Louvre Paris/Gianni Dagli Orti), 35 (Gianni Dagli Orti), 36
(Museo Prenestino Palestrina/Collection Dagli Orti), 38 (Musée du
Louvre Paris/Gianni Dagli Orti). • Getty Images: 26–27 (De Agostini/
Getty Images), 28 (De Agostini/Getty Images). • The Kobal Collection:
44 (Dreamworks/Universal). • shutterstock.com: 1 (Sean Nel), 4
(Timur Kulgarin), 5 (edobric), 6 (Kamira), 7 (iofoto), 8–9 (Motordigitaal),
11 (Only Fabrizio), 12 (Only Fabrizio), 15 (Caligula), 18 (Aaron Wood),
21 (Vilor), 23t (Mikhail Nekrasov), 23r (kated), 24 (Danilo Ascione), 27
(Diane Cramer), 30l (Anirudh's Magic Eye), 33b (Isabella Pfenninger),
34t (Lagui), 37m (Lagui), 37 (Ariy), 39 (Kamira), 40t (c.), 40b (meirion
matthias), 41b (Waj), 41r (Gary Blakeley), 42r (Lack-O'Keen), 42br
(ernstc), 43r (Oleg Golovnev), 44t (Victorian Traditions). • Topfoto (The
Granger Collection): 20, 30r, 34r; (topfoto.co.uk): 5, 18, 23, 25 (Roger-
Viollet), 31, 43b. • Werner Forman Archive: 13.

This book was produced for Crabtree Publishing Company
by Bender Richardson White

Library and Archives Canada Cataloguing in Publication

Johnson, Robin (Robin R.)
 Understanding Roman myths / Robin Johnson.

(Myths understood)
Includes index.
Issued also in electronic formats.
ISBN 978-0-7787-4510-5 (bound).--ISBN 978-0-7787-4515-0 (pbk.)

 1. Mythology, Roman--Juvenile literature. 2. Rome--Religion--
Juvenile literature. I. Title. II. Series: Myths understood

BL803.J64 2012   j292.1'30937   C2011-908373-6

Library of Congress Cataloging-in-Publication Data

Johnson, Robin (Robin R.)
 Understanding Roman myths / Robin Johnson.
  p. cm. -- (Myths understood)
 Includes index.
 ISBN 978-0-7787-4510-5 (reinforced library binding : alk.
paper) -- ISBN 978-0-7787-4515-0 (pbk. : alk. paper) -- ISBN
978-1-4271-7903-6 (electronic pdf) -- ISBN 978-1-4271-8018-6
(electronic html)
 1. Mythology, Roman--Juvenile literature. 2. Rome--
Religion--Juvenile literature. I. Title.

BL803.J656 2012
292.1'30937--dc23
                                        2011050093

Crabtree Publishing Company

www.crabtreebooks.com   1-800-387-7650

Printed in the U.S.A./022013/SN20130115

Published in Canada
Crabtree Publishing
616 Welland Ave.
St. Catharines, Ontario
L2M 5V6

Published in the United States
Crabtree Publishing
PMB 59051
350 Fifth Avenue, 59th Floor
New York, New York 10118

Published in the United Kingdom
Crabtree Publishing
Maritime House
Basin Road North, Hove
BN41 1WR

Published in Australia
Crabtree Publishing
3 Charles Street
Coburg North
VIC 3058

CONTENTS

WHAT ARE MYTHS? 4
What are myths and how do Roman myths relate to
the modern world? Vergil and Ovid—Roman poets
who wrote about legends and beliefs of the time.

ANCIENT ROME 6
The history of Rome from its founding in 753 B.C.E.
The creation of the Roman Empire, its laws,
traditions, art, and architecture.

RELIGION AND GODS 12
The pantheon of Roman gods and goddesses. Myths
about the creation of the world, gossiping, and
worshipping the gods.

THE NATURAL WORLD 18
The importance of agriculture and the gods and
myths associated with it. Myths about farming,
vanity, respecting the gods, and protecting Earth.

CLASSES OF PEOPLE 24
The daily life of Ancient Rome and the many myths
and legends related to it. Myths about patron gods,
strength and courage, marriage, arts and crafts.

TRAVEL AND WARFARE 34
The importance of travel and warfare in building
and keeping the empire. Myths about travelers, and
courage, duty, and loyalty to Rome and the emperors.

ROMAN LEGACY 40
How Ancient Roman culture, myths, and beliefs
remain alive today in movies, language, literature,
architecture, coins, and the calendar.

Time Chart   45

Glossary   46

Learning More   47

Index   48

WHAT ARE MYTHS?

Myths are traditional stories that are considered sacred or special to a group of people. Myths usually explore the early history of a culture. **They almost always include** supernatural **events or beings, such as gods and goddesses. People share myths and pass them down from one generation to the next in books, plays, poems, songs, and art.**

Myths are different from legends and fables. Legends are traditional stories about a single person or event. Legends seem as though they might be true stories, but cannot be proven by facts. Fables are stories, often with animals, that are meant to teach important lessons.

Myths also teach lessons, but they serve many other purposes as well. They explain the unknown, such as how the world began or how people were created. Myths give meaning to great or tragic events, such as plentiful crops or deadly floods. They explain the natural world, such as the reason for seasons and the origin of plants and stars. Roman myths served all of these purposes in ancient times and are still present in international cultures today.

VERGIL AND OVID

Vergil and Ovid were great Roman poets. They wrote many important works during the early days of the Roman Empire. They are most famous for their epic poems. An epic poem is a long poem that describes a country's early heroes and their adventures.

Vergil's most famous work is *The Aeneid*. It describes the difficult journey of a Trojan hero named Aeneas, who travels to Italy to start the Roman race of people. In the poem, Romulus, Jupiter, Juno, and many other key figures in Roman mythology appear.

Ovid's most popular work is called *Metamorphoses*. It features the gods and goddesses of Ancient Rome and their fascinating stories. The poem begins with the creation of Earth and continues to the death of Roman leader Julius Caesar.

Although also Vergil and Ovid wrote about the early history of Rome, their works taught Romans lessons about morality and their own lives. The poets also used myths to express their sometimes negative views about the Roman society they experienced.

Right: In this **mosaic** from 19 B.C.E., the poet Vergil is seated between the goddesses of history (holding a scroll) and tragedy (holding a mask).

Below: This statue from 1599 C.E. shows the Roman **demigod** Hercules slaying a mythical creature called a *centaur.*

ROMAN MYTHS

Roman myths taught the people of Rome about morality, or what is right and wrong. Myths showed Romans that good behaviors, such as hospitality and loyalty, would be rewarded. They warned Romans that greed, selfishness, and other bad behaviors would be punished. Myths showed Romans that duty, strength, and courage were vital in a nation that was constantly at war. Above all, myths taught Romans to honor, fear, and respect their gods—and their leaders.

ANCIENT ROME

Rome was an ancient civilization that became a mighty empire **more than 2,000 years ago. It began as a small farming community and grew into a rich and powerful city. Rome fought other nations and conquered their people. It grew to become the largest and greatest empire in the world at that time.**

In Italy, ancient peoples built small settlements on a group of hills. They lived in wooden huts and herded sheep and cattle. Over time, people from each hill came together and formed the city of Rome. The area where they lived was called the Seven Hills of Rome. It formed the geographic center of the ancient city.

BUILDING ROME

Early Romans learned how to build their city from their neighbors, the **Etruscans** and Greeks. Romans improved the building methods of other nations, however, and invented many new technologies. For example, Romans used concrete to construct large buildings quickly and cheaply. They also built long bridges called *aqueducts* to bring fresh water to the city.

ROMULUS AND REMUS

Historians believe Rome began as a small settlement between 800 B.C.E. and 700 B.C.E. According to the popular Roman founding myth, though, the city was created on April 21, 753 B.C.E., by twin brothers Romulus and Remus.

Romulus and Remus were twin baby boys who were thrown into a river because of their mother's crimes. The brothers were rescued by a wolf, who fed them with her milk. Then a poor shepherd discovered Romulus and Remus and raised them as his own. Over time, the boys grew into strong and brave young men. They decided to start a city, but argued over control of it. The brothers fought and Remus was killed. Romulus went on to **found** the city of Rome, which was named in his honor.

Above: A map of the Roman republic and main towns around 200 B.C.E.

Left: This bronze sculpture shows a wolf nursing twin brothers Romulus and Remus. Romulus became the first king of Rome and ruled the mighty city for 40 years.

Map labels:
- GAUL (FRANCE)
- YUGOSLAVIA
- Aquelia
- Mutina
- Bononia
- Ariminum
- Florentia
- Arezzo
- ADRIATIC SEA
- CORSICA
- Sutrium
- ROME
- Capua
- Brundisium
- Mt. Vesuvius and Pompeii
- SARDINIA
- TYRRHENIAN SEA
- Rhegium
- SICILY
- ROMAN REPUBLIC
- Main roads and trade routes
- 100 Miles
- 100 Kilometers
- N

THE ROMAN REPUBLIC

Rome became a republic in 509 B.C.E. A republic is a system of government in which certain people elect a small group of representatives. In the Roman republic each year, male citizens elected magistrates, including two consuls. The consuls were heads of the Roman government and the army. They were advised by the Senate, an unelected group of rich and powerful men who oversaw foreign relations, finances, and the official state religion.

The Roman republic lasted for nearly 500 years. During that time, the city of Rome grew into a powerful nation. The Roman army took control of Italy, then began to conquer other foreign peoples, such as the Carthaginians in North Africa and the Macedonians near Greece. The Romans believed they were helping the people they conquered by bringing order and civilized ways to them.

JULIUS CAESAR

Julius Caesar was a Roman general and consul who successfully conquered Gaul (France). In 49 B.C.E., Caesar started a **civil war** and took control of Rome.

LINK TO TODAY

From time to time, we hear modern stories of lost or abandoned children or injured explorers who have been looked after by wild animals or learned to survive with their help of wild animals. So the story of Romulus and Remus and the wolf is not completely unbelievable.

TWELVE TABLES

In 451 B.C.E., Romans created the Twelve Tables. These listed the laws of Rome that, until then, had not been explained clearly to most people. The tables formed the basis of Rome's legal system for almost 1,000 years.

He made many changes to improve Roman society. Caesar revised the Roman calendar (see page 43). He drained water from farmland and gave public land to soldiers and poor people. Caesar was very popular with the poor, but rich citizens feared he had become too powerful. In 44 B.C.E., noblemen killed Caesar to save the Roman republic. That system of government would never return to Rome, however.

Below: The Forum was the center of public life in the Roman republic. Many of its buildings used rows of tall columns to support the roof. Today, the Forum lies in ruins but can be visited and explored.

(see page 43)

KING TARQUIN

The myth of Tarquin and the sibyl warned Romans that too much power was a dangerous thing. It also showed them that the future of Rome was in their hands—if only they had the faith to believe it.

Tarquin the Proud was the seventh and final king of Rome. He was a foolish leader who never listened to his people. He did not listen to the Cumaean sibyl, either. A sibyl was a holy woman known for her ability to predict the future. The Cumaean sibyl visited King Tarquin and offered to sell him nine books that told the future of Rome. Tarquin laughed at the old woman, and she angrily burned three of the books. The sibyl offered him the remaining six books for the same price. The king proudly refused them again and the sibyl burned three more books. Finally, Tarquin agreed to buy the last three books.

Later, Romans studied the sibyl's books for solutions to the city's problems. Whenever they could not find the answers they needed, they blamed Tarquin for carelessly allowing the future of Rome to be burned. They grew angry at the king, rebelled against the monarchy, and Rome became a republic.

THE ROMAN EMPIRE

In 27 B.C.E., Augustus Caesar became the first emperor of Rome. An emperor is the supreme ruler of an empire. In Ancient Rome, the emperor made the laws and had absolute power. He was also the high priest and leader of the army.

Augustus was a wise and fair leader. He improved Roman society and brought peace to the nation (see page 38). After Augustus, a series of emperors took control. Some emperors, such as Trajan, Hadrian, and Marcus Aurelius, were wise, fair, and good. Other emperors were foolish, hungry for power, or even a little mad. Nero murdered his own mother, and Caligula planned to make his horse a consul! There were 66 Roman emperors in all. They conquered many nations and introduced their ways of life to the foreign lands. The emperors ruled Rome until the fall of much of the empire in 476 C.E.

ATTIS AND CYBELE

Attis and Cybele were deities (gods and goddesses) worshiped in Phrygia, a kingdom in modern-day Turkey. Romans conquered Phrygia and adopted their gods and the myth of Attis and Cybele.

An Earth goddess named Cybele fell in love with a handsome young shepherd named Attis. Attis promised to be true to Cybele, but then decided to marry a beautiful princess instead. Cybele was hurt and angry, so she drove Attis mad. Attis ran into the woods, wounded himself, and bled to death. Cybele transformed his body into a sacred pine tree, and violets grew from his spilled blood.

SHARING CULTURES

As the empire grew, the people conquered by Rome were forced to obey Roman laws, use Roman coins, and pay taxes to Rome. Many of them also adopted Roman customs. They began speaking Latin, the Roman language. They dressed like the Roman people, and built Roman-style buildings and roads.

Romans also learned from foreign peoples and brought new ideas, traditions, and cultures back to Rome. Romans were influenced by the architecture, writing, social systems, and art of the people they conquered. Many Romans learned to speak Greek. At the same time, the people of Rome learned of new gods and goddesses, and blended them and their myths into their religion and ways of life. Most of the new deities came from nearby Greece, but some came from faraway Egypt and Persia.

Above: This Roman shield was made around 450 C.E. It shows foreign deities Cybele and Attis riding in a chariot pulled by lions.

Right: Emperor Hadrian was a good ruler who strengthened Rome's defenses and improved life for the poor. His image is captured in this bronze statue.

EAST MEETS WEST

Mithra and Isis were foreign deities who became very popular in Rome. Mithra was a god from Persia (now Iran) that the Romans called Mithras. Roman soldiers worshiped the god because they believed he brought light and order to darkness and conflict. Isis was the Egyptian goddess of motherhood and nature. Romans worshiped Isis and believed she used magic to protect them from harm.

RELIGION *AND* GODS

Religion was very important to the Romans. They built magnificent temples for their gods and goddesses to live in. They prayed to the gods several times each day. They also burned incense, **gave gifts to the gods, and held many great festivals to honor them.**

By 146 B.C.E., Rome had conquered the people of Greece and discovered their gods and goddesses. Greek gods had colorful personalities and fascinating myths. Romans adopted the Greek gods, but renamed them to make them their own (see list, right). The gods and goddesses from Greece became the foundation of Roman religion. The 12 most important deities were called the *Dii Consentes*, or Roman Council of Gods (see chart). They were the most powerful gods and goddesses in the Roman **pantheon**, or collection of deities.

JUPITER AND JUNO

Jupiter was king of the gods and the supreme deity. Romans believed he controlled the sky, thunder, and laws of the land. He could change shape, throw his voice, and control lightning bolts. In fact, Jupiter had more power than any other Roman god. Jupiter was afraid of no one—except his jealous wife! Juno was queen of the gods. She controlled women, marriage, and motherhood. She also tried to control Jupiter, but that was difficult. The personalities of deities and people were very similar!

ROMAN vs. GREEK DEITIES

GREEK GODS	ROMAN GODS
Zeus	Jupiter
Ares	Mars
Apollo	Apollo
Poseidon	Neptune
Hermes	Mercury
Hephaestus	Vulcan

GREEK GODDESSES	ROMAN GODDESSES
Hera	Juno
Aphrodite	Venus
Artemis	Diana
Athena	Minerva
Demeter	Ceres
Hestia	Vesta

LARA AND MERCURY

The myth of Lara and Mercury told Romans to worship, fear, and respect the almighty gods. It also taught people—particularly women—that silence is a **virtue**, or a good thing.

Lara was a lovely little **nymph** with a big problem—she could not stop talking. She chatted from morning till night, gossiping and telling secrets about the gods. One day, Lara told Juno that her husband Jupiter had a girlfriend—a goddess named Juturna. Jupiter was furious that Lara had carelessly revealed his secret, so he cut off Lara's tongue. Then he ordered Mercury to take Lara to the **underworld**. Along the way, however, Mercury fell in love with the beautiful and silent nymph. He did not take her to the underworld. Instead he had children with her. Mercury and Lara were afraid that Jupiter might harm their children—known simply as Lares, or Lara's children—so they made them invisible and sent them away to live with **mortals**.

HOUSEHOLD GODS

Families in Ancient Rome worshiped household gods called *Lares*. They prayed to the gods at small **shrines** inside their homes. They also put Lares statues on their dinner tables and offered them honey cakes, grapes, wine, and other gifts to please them and win favor. In return, Lares guarded people's homes and protected them from harm.

Left: Romans worshiped household gods at shrines called *lorariums.* This ancient lararium was found in a home in Pompeii.

GODS OF DAILY LIFE

The people of Rome worshiped hundreds of gods and goddesses. Romans believed that gods watched over every aspect of their lives. The gods controlled marriage, children, crops, cooking, the weather, seas, victory in war, love, and everything else that mattered to Romans.

The 12 main Roman deities lived far away from people at the top of Mount Olympus in Greece. Romans believed that many other gods lived all around them. Some gods lived outdoors. They protected forests, hills, rivers, and other parts of nature. Other gods lived indoors. They lived in people's cupboards, kitchens, fireplaces, and throughout their homes. The entrance to a Roman home was guarded by three separate gods! One god protected the door sill or steps, another god protected the door hinges, and a third protected the door itself.

Above: Romans perform a sacred ceremony to the gods in this mosaic from 80 B.C.E.

TEMPLES

Romans worshiped their gods at temples throughout the empire. Some temples were small, while others were huge buildings. The most important gods had the most impressive temples. Roman priests guarded the temples and performed ceremonies and rituals there. Rituals are special religious actions that are always done the same way.

AUGURS

Some high priests were known as *augurs*. Augurs tried to tell the future and understand the wishes of the gods and goddesses. They studied the behaviors of birds in the sky to find signs from the gods. Roman leaders always consulted augurs before they started wars or made important decisions for Rome.

DEUCALION AND PYRRHA

Romans believed that Earth began in a state of chaos—a shapeless mass of confusion. Then a creator god made the heavens and Earth. He separated land from sea and added mountains, valleys, lakes, rivers, and trees. He filled the sky with gods and stars and created people to rule Earth.

In the beginning, people were honorable and good. They led simple, peaceful lives. Over time, however, people became violent, greedy, and evil. They began to fight wars and abuse Earth. The god Jupiter decided to destroy the human race to make the world safer for gods, nymphs, and other **divine** beings. He sent a great flood to Earth, destroying everything and drowning nearly all the people. Only a man named Deucalion and his wife Pyrrha survived the flood because they were **pious** and good. They begged the gods to help them rebuild the human race. The goddess Themis took pity on the lone couple and told them to throw stones behind them. Deucalion and Pyrrha did so and then watched in amazement as the stones slowly transformed into people. The couple threw stone after stone and gradually repopulated Earth.

Above: The Pantheon, with its columned entrance, was a home for the deities of myths and a feat of Roman engineering built with strong columns.

LINK TO TODAY

The Pantheon was a grand temple for all the gods and goddesses of Ancient Rome. It was built in 27 B.C.E., then rebuilt in 126 C.E. Nearly 2,000 years later, the Pantheon remains one of the largest domes in the world—and one of the most impressive temples ever built.

MORTALITY AND DEATH

Many Romans died at an early age. They lived in crowded, dirty conditions where diseases spread quickly. They did not have modern medicines or nutritious foods to eat. Babies often died at birth. Parents put unwanted babies outside and left them to die. Many children also died from diseases.

Romans buried the dead in cemeteries outside the city walls. It was against the law for the dead to be buried inside the city, because dead bodies were considered unclean for religious reasons. Funerals usually took place at night. A solemn funeral procession—made up of family members, musicians, and torch bearers—

Below: On this carving, Romans mourn the death of a loved one killed by a disease that swept through Rome from 165 to 180 C.E.

carried the body to a cemetery for burial. Children were often buried with their dolls, marbles, tops, or other favorite toys. Wealthy Romans were buried in fine **tombs** along the side of the road. The bodies of the poorest Romans and slaves were buried together in large pits.

CROSSING THE STYX

Romans believed that when people died, their souls went to the underworld. The underworld was the kingdom of the dead. To reach the underworld, the dead had to cross the imaginary River Styx. Romans put coins in the mouths of their dead loved ones so they could pay the fee to cross the Styx, and reach their eternal resting place.

Romans also cremated the dead—they burned the bodies to ashes. When Romans cremated their loved ones, they threw food and clothes into the fire for the dead to use in the afterlife. Romans commonly kept the ashes of the dead in stone or clay containers called *urns*. The urns were carved with special words and pictures then stored in family tombs or buried in cemeteries.

Left: Orpheus charms the animals with his lyre in this Roman mosaic from between 200 and 300 C.E. A lyre is a stringed instrument similar to a harp.

ORPHEUS AND EURYDICE

The myth of Orpheus and Eurydice shows that worshiping the gods was a matter of life and death for the Romans. It told people to trust and obey their gods—or the results would be eternally tragic.

Orpheus was a talented musician who made enchanting music with his lyre. He married a lovely young nymph named Eurydice. On their wedding day, Eurydice was bitten by a poisonous snake. She died instantly and was taken to the underworld. Orpheus could not bear to lose his beautiful new bride, so he descended to the underworld to rescue her. He played his lyre and charmed the guards and gods of the dead. They agreed to release Eurydice, but with one condition: Orpheus had to walk in front of his wife and could not look back at her until they had returned to Earth. Orpheus agreed and led Eurydice out of the darkness. They had almost reached the land of the living when Orpheus began to wonder if his wife was still behind him. Disobeying the gods, he turned to look at Eurydice—and she disappeared forever.

THE NATURAL WORLD

Romans believed that the natural world was a gift from the gods. The natural world includes trees, flowers, and animals. Romans worshiped the gods who controlled the natural world and hoped they would bless Rome with plenty of animals to hunt and crops to harvest.

Agriculture was very important to Romans. It was the biggest industry in Ancient Rome. Most Romans lived and worked on farms throughout the empire. They rose early and worked long, hard days to produce the food and materials that Rome's cities needed to grow.

GROWING AN EMPIRE

Roman farmers produced many crops. They grew foods that were suited to the hot, dry climate of Rome. Farmers grew cereal crops, such as wheat, oats, barley, and rye. They grew olives for making oil and grapes for making wine. Farmers also raised cattle, sheep, pigs, and goats. They used the animals for their meat, milk, and wool. They also used the hides, or skins, of the animals to make leather goods.

PRAYING FOR CROPS

Roman farmers prayed for their crops to grow. They worshiped Saturn, Ops, and Ceres, the main gods and goddesses of agriculture. They also worshiped countless other gods who controlled the planting of seeds, plowing, and harvesting. They even worshiped a goddess who made ears of corn grow evenly!

LINK TO TODAY

Romans called wine *vinum*. This is the source of the English words "wine" and "vine"—the type of plant on which grapes grow.

Below: After working in the fields, farmers enjoyed food and wine. They were served from jars at snack bars, such as this one in the ancient town of Pompeii.

LIBER AND FALERNUS

The Liber and Falernus myth highlights the importance of farming in Ancient Rome—especially viticulture, or growing grapes. It also shows that hospitality and kindness were necessary virtues, or good qualities, in a growing empire.

Liber was god of the countryside, grapes, and wine. One hot day, he visited an old farmer named Falernus. Falernus was very poor, but especially kind. Without even asking the stranger his name, Falernus generously offered him food to eat and water to drink. Liber accepted the meal, but refused the water. (He was the god of wine, after all.) Instead, Liber shared with the thirsty farmer his own jug of wine. Falernus had never tasted wine so good! He drank glass after glass, but Liber's jug never emptied. Finally, Falernus fell asleep. When he woke up the next morning, his fields were filled with ripening grapevines, stretching in rows as far as the eye could see. Liber had rewarded Falernus for his hospitality by giving him more grapes than he and his fellow villagers would ever need.

NECTAR OF THE GODS

There was no coffee or tea in Ancient Rome so everyone from slaves to emperors drank wine or clean water. Roman farmers grew grapes in vineyards and picked them carefully by hand. Then they stomped on the grapes and used the juice to make wine.

Left: Romans grew grapes throughout the empire. This mosaic from around 150 C.E. shows Romans working in vineyards in North Africa.

PLANTS AND ANIMALS

Plants and animals were a big part of Roman life. Romans visited public flower gardens in the city. Wealthy Romans had their own gardens in **courtyards**. Romans kept dogs, birds, and other animals as pets. Plants and animals also had many practical uses in Ancient Rome, however.

PRACTICAL PLANTS

Romans used **herbs**, flowers, and other plants to make medicines, perfumes, and makeup. They also used herbs to season foods. Romans used mint to flavor wines and sauces, but they also used it to improve digestion and cure coughs and colds. Romans grew mint, rosemary, thyme, fennel, and many other herbs in country gardens. They also **imported** herbs from the East.

LINK TO TODAY

Flora was the Roman goddess of flowers. She made flowers bloom when she played her sweet music. Faunus was a god of fields and forests who was half man and half goat. The English words *flora* and *fauna* come from their names. The flora is all the plants that grow in an area, and the fauna is all the animals that live there.

Below: This mosaic from 325 C.E. shows Romans hunting wild animals. Wealthy Roman men hunted deer, foxes, wild boars, rabbits, and other animals for sport and food.

ECHO AND NARCISSUS

The myth of Echo and Narcissus gave Romans the origin of a beautiful flower species. It also explained the phenomenon of echoes and warned people that being talkative or vain—believing you are great when you are not—would reflect poorly on Rome.

Echo was a lively young mountain nymph who was very talkative. She had been punished for her chatter by the goddess Juno, so Echo could only repeat the last words that others spoke. Echo fell in love with a handsome and vain young hunter named Narcissus. Narcissus cruelly rejected Echo and she faded away from sadness until only her voice remained in the hills. One day, Narcissus was tired from hunting deer. He stopped to drink from a cool stream and noticed his own reflection in the water. He instantly fell in love with his shimmering image. Narcissus stared at himself for days and days until, like Echo, he faded away. In his place, a lovely Narcissus flower grew at the water's edge.

ROMAN BEASTS

Romans used animals for both work and play. Farmers used donkeys and oxen to pull wagons, plows, and other heavy farm equipment. Wealthy men hunted wild animals for sport. Slaves fought lions, tigers, bears, elephants, and other exotic animals in public shows (see page 30). Romans brought many thousands of wild animals from faraway lands to kill in their sporting games.

LINK TO TODAY

Narcissus flowers were named for the mythical youth, Narcissus. They often grow near water and face downward, as Narcissus did to see his reflection in the water. The word *narcissistic* also comes from Narcissus. It describes people who admire themselves and the way they look.

ANIMAL SACRIFICES

Romans also sacrificed animals as part of religious rituals. To sacrifice is to kill an animal as a gift to the gods. Romans often sacrificed pigs, bulls, and sheep. Priests examined the insides of the dead animals for signs that the gods were pleased. If any body part was diseased or injured, a new animal would be sacrificed. Priests also inspected the insides to predict the future.

HEAVEN AND EARTH

Romans believed the gods controlled the weather, the seasons, and everything to do with the atmosphere and Earth. People worshiped the gods to keep them happy.

When the gods were very pleased, the weather was fine and people were safe. When the gods were angry or jealous, they punished people for their actions. Romans explained every snowfall, storm, and natural disaster—including hurricanes, volcanoes, and earthquakes—as messages from angry gods. When the sky god Jupiter was angry, he threw lightning bolts and sent violent thunderstorms to shake the land. When Neptune, god of the sea, was

THE FALL OF PHAETHON

Romans believed the gods also controlled the Sun, Moon, stars, and everything else in the night sky and heavens far above. The myth of Phaethon reinforced this belief. It also taught Romans to respect their gods and protect Earth—and even predicted the future threat of global warming!

Apollo, god of the Sun, had a son named Phaethon. Phaethon lived on Earth with his mother Clymene. As he grew up, Phaethon began to wonder if he really was the son of the Sun god. One day, he climbed the steep path to Apollo's shiny palace in the sky to find out. Apollo promised his son one favor to prove his fatherly love. Phaethon immediately asked to drive Apollo's chariot of fire—the Sun—for one day. Apollo begged him to change his mind and choose anything other than the dangerous ride across the sky. Phaethon insisted, however, and his father reluctantly agreed. Apollo explained how to steer the winged horses and spread the Sun's light and warmth evenly around the world. Phaethon proudly took the reins and began his fateful journey. The inexperienced driver soon lost control of the golden chariot, however, and the horses began to run wild. They dipped low to the ground, scorching fields, drying up rivers, melting snow, and creating deserts. The whole Earth was on fire! When Jupiter could no longer bear the destruction, he hurled a lightning bolt at the chariot and killed young Phaethon.

unhappy, he flooded the land or sent stormy weather to ships at sea. Romans lived in constant fear of their gods and the terrible disasters they might send down to Earth.

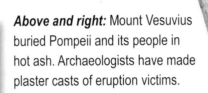

Above and right: Mount Vesuvius buried Pompeii and its people in hot ash. Archaeologists have made plaster casts of eruption victims.

NAMING PLANETS

Romans believed there were seven planets circling Earth—the Moon, the Sun, Mercury, Venus, Mars, Jupiter, and Saturn. They named the planets to honor their gods. For example, Jupiter is the biggest planet in the Solar System, so Romans named it for the king of the gods. Venus is the brightest planet in the night sky, so they named it for the goddess of beauty.

LINK TO TODAY

In 79 C.E., Mount Vesuvius in Italy erupted. No one realized that earthquakes had signaled the coming disaster. Over the course of two days, the volcano completely buried the towns of Pompeii and Herculaneum in a thick layer of rock and hot ash. For centuries, the ash preserved the towns. Today, the ruins of the towns give visitors a rare glimpse of life, death, and natural disaster in Ancient Rome.

Below: Phaethon rode a chariot like the one in this mosaic from 300 C.E.

CLASSES OF PEOPLE

Roman society was based on a complex class system. Different people held different ranks, or positions in society. Having a high rank was very important to Romans. It earned them rights and respect. Class also determined their marriages, families, clothing, homes, education, and other parts of their daily lives.

There were three classes of citizen in Ancient Rome. Patricians were certain families with special privileges. Equestrians were people who had become wealthy in business. Plebeians were everybody else. Only men could vote in elections. Female citizens, and non-citizens such as foreigners, did not have the rights of male citizens, but they could run businesses.

SLAVES

Slaves held the lowest position in Roman society. They had no rights at all. Slaves were treated as property and were bought and sold by the **free**. They worked hard for their owners and were often treated cruelly. Slaves who worked in mines, for the army, and on farms had short, miserable lives.

Above: Roman slaves serve wine in this stone **relief** from about 150 C.E.

THE SLAVE SPARTACUS

Spartacus was a Roman slave who led a revolt in 73 B.C.E. He escaped from a gladiator school and was soon joined by thousands of other slaves. They robbed villages and defeated Roman forces. Before the slaves could escape from Italy, soldiers caught them. Spartacus probably fought to the death, but many slaves were crucified.

THE WOMEN OF SABINE

The myth of the Sabine women highlights the classes of people in Rome and the importance of climbing the ancient social ladder. It also shows the necessity of marriage and family in even the earliest days of the civilization.

In the early history of Rome, there were few women in the city. Roman men needed women to take care of them and start families. Nearby tribes proudly refused to allow Romans to marry their women, so the Romans threw a great festival. They welcomed a tribe called the Sabines to their city. Then the Romans stole the young Sabine women, and attacked and drove the Sabine men from Rome. King Romulus promised the Sabine women that, if they married Roman men, they would have the rights of citizens and their children would be free. Although they were heartbroken and angry, the women reluctantly agreed. Later, the Sabine men returned and waged war on Rome. The women—who still loved their Sabine fathers but had also grown to love their Roman husbands—stepped between the two armies. The armies declared a truce, and the Sabine men became citizens of Rome.

They did backbreaking work and were kept in chains so they could not escape. Household slaves had more comforts, especially if they belonged to rich owners.

BIRTHRIGHTS

A person's position in society was determined at birth. Children belonged to the same class as their parents. Slaves could buy their freedom or be freed by their owners as a reward for loyal service. Plebeians and freed slaves could also improve their places in society by becoming rich and successful.

Below: These wealthy ladies were found on a wall painting in the Ancient Roman town of Pompeii.

FAMILY LIFE

Family was the foundation of Roman society. Members of a family cared for and protected one another. They prayed together, and often worked together in family shops or farms. Most Roman families were small, with only two or three children. Grandparents and other elderly relatives often lived with the family. Slaves lived with them, too.

The father was the head of the household. According to Roman law, his wife and children belonged to him. The father's duty was to protect and provide for his family. The mother's duty was to produce sons to carry on the family name and business. Romans believed that a woman's place was in the home. Mothers were in charge of the day-to-day lives of their families. They took care of the

Above: Many wealthy Roman families lived in country houses called *villas*. Villas often had small open pools and a kitchen garden to provide food.

children, prepared meals, cleaned, and ran the household. Poor mothers also helped support their families. They worked in shops, markets, or taverns. Wealthy mothers had slaves who took care of their children and homes for them.

LINK TO TODAY

The Ionian Sea was named after the mythical nymph Io (see page 27). It is the body of water between Italy and Greece that poor Io swam across to escape Juno's stinging fly.

ROMAN CLOTHING

Roman men wore knee-length, sleeveless garments called *tunics*. Citizens were also allowed to wear *togas*. Togas were long woollen robes that men wore on special occasions. Women wore long, loose gowns called *stolas* and wrapped shawls over their heads and shoulders. Children wore the same types of clothes as their parents, but in smaller sizes.

ROMAN MARRIAGE

Roman marriages were arranged by families. Parents chose partners for their children based on money and social status. Girls were allowed to marry when they were 12 years old. Boys could marry when they were 14. The wedding ceremony took place in the bride's home. Family and friends gathered to watch the couple exchange vows, then everyone enjoyed a feast. The bride lived in her husband's home—and sometimes even grew to love him.

JUPITER, JUNO, AND IO

This myth illustrates a typical Roman marriage. Although men had legal power over their wives, women often wore the pants—or tunics—in the family.

Jupiter, king of the gods and heavens, fell in love with a beautiful river nymph named Io. He filled the sky with thick clouds so his wife Juno could not see them together. Juno was suspicious of Jupiter, though, so he quickly changed Io into a little white cow. Juno was not fooled by her husband's trick. She asked Jupiter to give her the cow as a gift. Then Juno ordered Argus, a giant with a hundred eyes, to guard the cow. Jupiter sent Mercury to rescue Io. Mercury played music and told Argus a long story to lull the giant to sleep. Then Mercury killed Argus and freed Io. When Juno realized the cow had escaped, she sent a stinging fly after her. Poor Io swam across a sea and fled in madness all the way to Egypt to avoid the fly and the wrath of jealous Juno.

Left: A Roman bride and groom enjoy their wedding feast in this 3rd-century C.E. relief.

THE GEESE AND THE GAULS

Romans believed their city was guarded by patron gods. Patron gods protect a particular person or place from harm. Romans worshiped the patron gods of Rome, including Juno, Jupiter, and Minerva. In return, Romans trusted the gods to warn them of danger and keep their city safe, especially in times of war.

One night, the Gauls invaded Rome. Hidden in the dark, armed soldiers quietly snuck up Capitoline Hill toward the sleeping Roman guards. Before the Gauls reached the top of the hill, however, a flock of angry geese attacked them. The geese pecked at the intruders and hit them with their wings. The commotion woke the Roman guards, who quickly prepared to defend the city. The Romans believed that the patron goddess Juno—whose sacred animal was the goose—had alerted the guards and helped protect Rome.

Right: Streets in Roman towns and cities were busy places. Homeowners often had workshops or stalls that opened onto the street. Animal-drawn carts carried goods along the paved highway.

CITY LIFE

The city of Rome was a busy place! The narrow noisy streets were filled with vendors selling goods, and people hurrying from place to place. There were many shops, markets, and taverns. There were also many large, beautiful temples, theaters, public baths, and other buildings.

PUBLIC BATHS

Romans visited public baths several times a week. A public bath was made up of hot and cold pools, as well as exercise areas and gardens. Romans visited the baths to wash, play sports and games, and relax.

THE FORUM

The Forum (see page 8–9) was the heart of Ancient Rome. It was a huge open space in the center of the city. Romans gathered there to watch parades and religious ceremonies, and to hear speeches by their leaders. Surrounding the Forum were important public buildings, such as temples, law courts, and the Senate House.

Above: In this 3rd century C.E. mosaic, Roman slaves help dress a man at the public baths.

They also met their friends there, because most Roman homes were too small for guests.

ROMAN HOMES

Most Romans lived in cramped, dirty rooms in crumbling six-story apartment buildings. The rooms were cold and damp in winter, hot in summer, and crowded all year long. They had no running water or toilets. People got their water from public fountains and threw their waste down drains—or right out the windows!

Most homes did not have kitchens. People bought food at markets, food stands, and bakeries in the city. Rich Romans had kitchens and slaves to prepare their meals. They ate fine foods in fancy dining rooms.

Wealthy families lived in town houses. They had large rooms and lovely private gardens. Some rich families also had villas, or charming country homes. The villas had gardens, orchards, and pools. The walls and floors of the villas were decorated with beautiful painted plasterwork and mosaics.

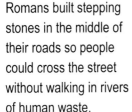

Right and below: Romans built stepping stones in the middle of their roads so people could cross the street without walking in rivers of human waste.

Romans loved sports and games. They rode horses, wrestled, and played dice games. They also gathered by the thousands to see daring displays of skill, strength, and courage. Gladiator contests and chariot races were the most popular public events in Ancient Rome.

GLADIATOR CONTESTS

Gladiators were slaves, prisoners, and other men who fought to the death in savage hand-to-hand combat. They faced other fierce gladiators—and even wild animals! Some gladiators were armed with spears, swords, or nets. Some wore helmets and body armor and carried shields for protection. Other gladiators had no weapons or armor, and fought with their bare hands.

LINK TO TODAY

Romans gathered in huge stadiums to watch shows of all kinds. They watched gladiator contests, mock sea battles, plays, and other performances in open-air arenas called *amphitheaters*. The Colosseum (below) was the largest and greatest amphitheater in Ancient Rome. It held up to 50,000 spectators!

GLADIATOR

Commodus was a cruel emperor who wanted Romans to see him as the mythical hero Hercules. Commodus had statues made of himself dressed as Hercules. He also fought as a gladiator to show his strength to the Roman people. But he actually only fought wounded people and tame animals so he could win.

Above: The gladiators in this Roman mosaic are prepared to fight to the death.

HERCULES AND CACUS

Roman men were prized for their strength and courage in gladiator contests, chariot races, and many other arenas. The demigod Hercules was a model for their behavior. Hercules was half man, half god, and all muscle! He was known for his incredible strength, bravery, and persistence. Hercules accomplished many difficult tasks and earned the respect of both gods and mortals.

One day, Hercules was herding cattle through the countryside of Italy. When he stopped to rest in a grassy meadow, Cacus stole some of his finest oxen. Cacus was a giant fire-breathing half-human monster who lived on human flesh. Cacus pulled the oxen backward by their tails into his cave, so their hoof prints would not reveal his crime. When Hercules awoke, he heard one of his stolen oxen lowing sadly inside the dark cave. He charged angrily toward the cave, but Cacus blocked the entrance with a huge boulder. Hercules could not move the heavy rock, so he tore away at the mountainside and opened the roof of the cave. He threw trees and rocks down at Cacus. Then Hercules jumped into the cave, grabbed Cacus around his giant neck, and squeezed until the eyes popped out of the vile monster's head.

Above: Some Roman gladiators wore helmets like this one for protection.

CHARIOT RACES

Chariot races were another popular event in Ancient Rome. A chariot is a small, light cart pulled by a team of horses. Thousands of fans cheered as daring drivers, called charioteers, raced at breakneck speed around oval tracks. Although winning charioteers became famous throughout Rome, the chariots often crashed. Many men and horses were killed or injured in the dangerous sport.

MINERVA AND ARACHNE

Romans believed that the gods influenced and inspired all art. Artists worshiped the gods and, in return, the gods guided artists to create beautiful works. The myth of Minerva and Arachne shows the importance of arts and crafts in Ancient Rome, as well as the danger of scorning the gods and their divine art lessons.

Arachne was a talented artist who was known throughout heaven and Earth for her stunning **tapestries**. One day, she boasted that she was a better weaver than Minerva, the goddess of arts and crafts. Arachne would not admit that Minerva had taught her or guided her art in any way. In fact, she boldly challenged the goddess to a weaving contest! Arachne created a beautiful tapestry that showed the gods behaving badly. Minerva was upset by Arachne's disrespectful design. She destroyed Arachne's tapestry and angrily hit her on the head with a weaving tool. Arachne tried to kill herself in shame but Minerva took pity on the poor mortal. She turned Arachne into a spider so she could continue to spin her heavenly art.

LEARNING AND EDUCATION

Latin was the official language of Rome. It was used in government, schools, temples, and courts of law. People spoke Latin throughout the empire, which allowed Romans to trade and communicate with people in distant lands. Although most Romans spoke Latin, few people could read or write. Only rich families could afford educations in Ancient Rome.

Wealthy boys and girls went to primary schools until they were 11 or 12 years old. They learned basic subjects, such as reading, writing, and math. Then girls stopped attending school so they could

Above: This 4th-century C.E. relief shows a Roman teacher and his students in class.

learn how to do housework and prepare for marriage. Girls often continued their studies at home. Boys continued their education at grammar schools. They studied history, geography, literature, law, and public speaking. Children from poor families did not attend school. They were forced to work for a living at an early age.

Above: Romans often featured mythical beings in their art, such as this wall mosaic of Neptune.

Above: Roman schoolchildren used materials like the writing tablets and bronze inkwell shown here.

ROMAN ART

Roman artists and craftspeople produced many incredible pieces of art. Romans were known in particular for their paintings, sculptures, glass vases, and mosaics. Mosaics are pictures made from tiny colored tiles arranged in a pattern. Most Roman artwork featured landscapes, people and animals, or scenes from Roman mythology.

Although some ancient works have survived, little is known about the artists who created them. Roman artists were considered tradespeople, and they rarely signed their work. It is clear, however, that Roman artists were influenced by the Greeks. Roman artists often copied Greek sculptures and other works they admired.

TRAVEL *AND* WARFARE

Romans traveled throughout the empire on a vast network of roads that connected cities to distant lands. The roads allowed Romans to travel quickly and easily, move armies, communicate, and trade goods with other nations.

The city of Rome produced few of the basic items it needed, so Romans imported goods or traded for them. Different parts of the empire produced different goods. For example, people in Sicily and North Africa produced grains, and people in Gaul and Spain made wine. Roman merchants traded with one another to get the items they needed. Merchants from Rome also got silk from China and spices and perfumes from India, outside the empire.

Merchants traveled in carts along Roman roads. They also traveled by ship across the Mediterranean Sea and other waters. Romans built deep wooden merchant ships to carry big loads of cargo. The ships were powered by sails, so Romans could only travel when the wind blew in the right direction. Sailors did not have compasses to guide them, so they often traveled within sight of land.

Above: Romans traveled by sea slowly in sturdy wooden ships like the ones in this copy of a 6th-century C.E. mosaic.

BAUCIS AND PHILEMON

Romans considered guests a blessing sent by the gods. They believed that travelers should always be treated with hospitality, generosity, and kindness, as demonstrated by Baucis and Philemon in this myth.

One day, Jupiter and Mercury disguised themselves as weary travelers. Looking for a place to rest, they visited a thousand homes and were rudely turned away by all the wealthy townspeople. Only a poor old couple named Baucis and Philemon took pity on them. They welcomed the travelers into their humble cottage and served them a simple but tasty meal. Then Jupiter and Mercury revealed they were gods, and took their kind hosts to the top of a mountain. They flooded the town below, killing all who lived there. The gods granted Baucis and Philemon one wish in return for their generosity—to die at the same time. When their lives were over, Baucis and Philemon were transformed into noble trees, standing together with their limbs entwined.

LINK TO TODAY

Romans were master road builders. They planned their routes carefully and made the roads straight and strong. Romans used layers of sand, gravel, and stones to make the roads, with ditches along the sides to drain water. Some Roman roads have been used for thousands of years—long after the fall of the empire.

Right: A Roman merchant's cart pulled by oxen, as shown in this mosaic from around 350 C.E.

SOLDIERS AND WARFARE

The Roman army was a powerful fighting force. It was made up of thousands of well-trained, well-organized, and well-armed soldiers. The soldiers fought many bloody battles as Rome waged war on other countries and increased its land.

The army consisted of units called *legions*. Each legion had about 5,000 foot soldiers. The soldiers wore helmets and chest armor and carried shields for protection. They fought with spears, swords, and daggers. Roman cavalry soldiers rode horses. The cavalry patrolled the battle area and fought alongside the foot soldiers. The Roman army also used large wooden war machines in battle. They used battering rams to break through enemy walls and gates. They used catapults to throw boulders, stones, huge darts, and thick arrows over walls.

Below: This mosaic from around 80 B.C.E. features a group of Roman soldiers on the River Nile in Egypt.

GATES OF JANUS

King Numa Pompilius ruled Rome from 715 to 673 B.C.E. He built a sacred temple to Janus, the god of doorways, gates, beginnings, and endings. The bronze temple doors—called the Gates of Janus—were to remain open during times of war and be closed during times of peace. During the peaceful reign of Numa, the Gates of Janus were kept closed. The next Roman king opened the gates, and they stayed open for 400 years! In fact, the gates were closed only once during the long and violent history of the Roman republic.

ARMY LIFE

Life in the Roman army was difficult. Soldiers endured tough training to become fierce fighting machines. They learned how to march, swim, ride horses, build forts and roads, and use a variety of weapons. They were often forced to walk long distances—up to 18 miles (29 kilometers) a day—carrying heavy loads. Soldiers were severely punished or killed if they disobeyed orders or dishonored their country. Despite the tough conditions, many Roman men joined the army. They were eager to learn useful skills and be paid to fight for Rome.

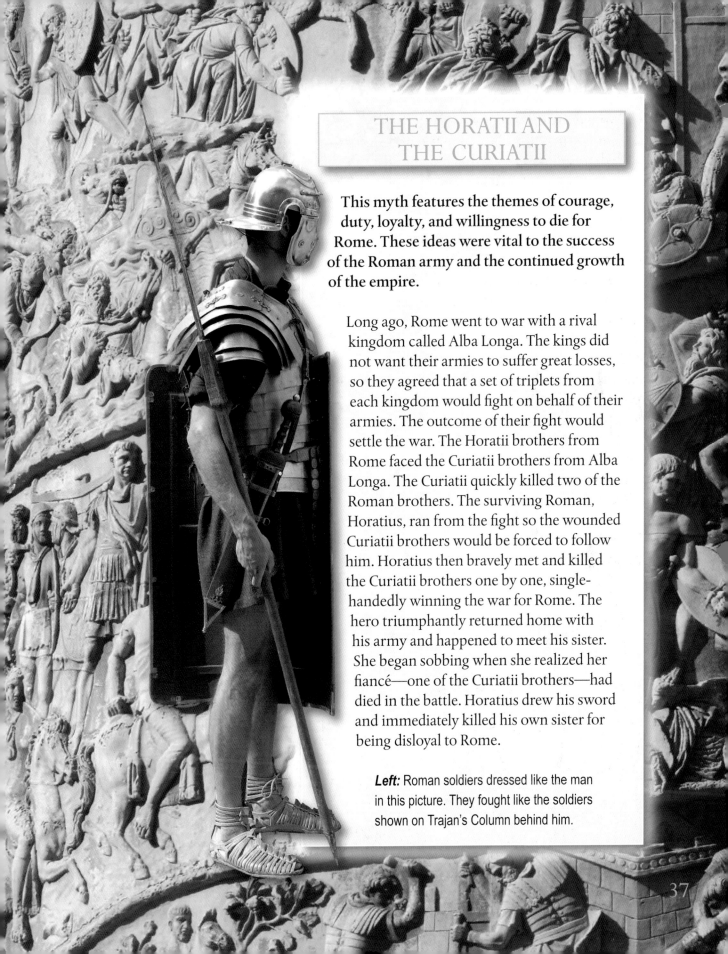

THE HORATII AND THE CURIATII

This myth features the themes of courage, duty, loyalty, and willingness to die for Rome. These ideas were vital to the success of the Roman army and the continued growth of the empire.

Long ago, Rome went to war with a rival kingdom called Alba Longa. The kings did not want their armies to suffer great losses, so they agreed that a set of triplets from each kingdom would fight on behalf of their armies. The outcome of their fight would settle the war. The Horatii brothers from Rome faced the Curiatii brothers from Alba Longa. The Curiatii quickly killed two of the Roman brothers. The surviving Roman, Horatius, ran from the fight so the wounded Curiatii brothers would be forced to follow him. Horatius then bravely met and killed the Curiatii brothers one by one, single-handedly winning the war for Rome. The hero triumphantly returned home with his army and happened to meet his sister. She began sobbing when she realized her fiancé—one of the Curiatii brothers—had died in the battle. Horatius drew his sword and immediately killed his own sister for being disloyal to Rome.

Left: Roman soldiers dressed like the man in this picture. They fought like the soldiers shown on Trajan's Column behind him.

In 27 B.C.E., Augustus became the first emperor of Rome. Augustus was Julius Caesar's great-nephew and adopted son. Like Caesar, Augustus was a popular leader. He improved Roman society and brought peace to the nation.

When Augustus took control of Rome, the country was in turmoil. Romans had been fighting civil wars for years. Augustus knew that Romans did not want to be ruled by a king, so he called himself simply the "first citizen." Augustus claimed that he had brought the republic back to Rome. The Senate had no real power at all, however. Augustus had total control of the Roman Empire.

Augustus successfully ruled Rome for more than 40 years. During that time, he made many changes and improvements to the country. Augustus reorganized the Roman army, increased its size, and turned it into a professional fighting force. He built roads and bridges throughout the empire. Augustus created many new colonies and traveled to distant lands to meet his people.

HOLY EMPERORS

When Augustus died in 14 C.E., he was *deified*. To deify is to give someone godly status and worship them as a supreme being. Many Roman emperors after Augustus were also deified. Some were declared gods while they were still living! Worshiping the emperors of Rome helped keep peace and order in the nation.

A PEACEFUL LIFE

Augustus convinced the people of Rome that peace was better than war. Although Rome continued to expand its empire under Augustus, Romans were united. Augustus brought order to the empire, and it lasted for more than 200 years. The long period of peace and prosperity was known as *Pax Romana*, or Roman Peace.

Left: Roman emperors Vespasian and Titus were deified when they died, as shown in this painting from 1537 C.E.

AENEAS'S EPIC JOURNEY

Emperor Augustus hired the poet Vergil to write an epic poem about the early history of Rome. The poem, called *The Aeneid*, featured a hero from Troy (in present-day Turkey) named Aeneas. It described the adventures of Aeneas on his long and tough journey to Italy, and tells how he became the heroic ancestor of the Roman people. This myth is part of his story.

Guided by a **prophecy**, Aeneas set sail with the survivors of the Trojan War. The goddess Juno disliked the Trojans—the people of Troy—so she meddled in their journey. She ordered the god of the winds to create a deadly storm with huge waves and powerful winds. Aeneas and his men were thrown off course and nearly drowned, but they boldly continued their quest for Italy. At last, the god Neptune stepped in to take control of the sea. He calmed the waters and rescued the ships, and Aeneas continued his journey. Aeneas went on to found the Italian city of Lavinium, which ultimately led to the founding of Rome.

REBUILDING ROME

Augustus also helped rebuild the city of Rome, which had been torn apart by civil wars. He built a new Forum, as well as many great marble temples and theaters. Augustus started police and fire departments to help protect his people. He repaired aqueducts—bridges for water—and built sewers to help people stay healthy. Augustus worked hard to turn Rome into a glorious city, and his work paid off.

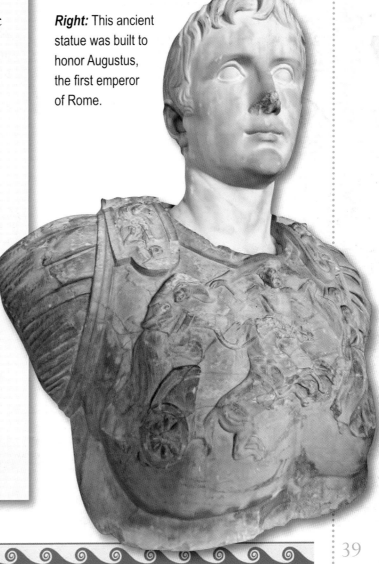

Right: This ancient statue was built to honor Augustus, the first emperor of Rome.

ROMAN LEGACY

Romans studied the Greeks, Etruscans, and other civilizations that came before them. The people of Rome were influenced by their ideas and achievements. Romans realized that learning from the past would help them expand their city and become a great nation. Today, we can follow the Roman example and learn about our own world by studying theirs.

Roman buildings, bridges, aqueducts, and roads were marvels of the ancient world. Many of their impressive structures are still standing today, many centuries after they were built. They are a clear and lasting **legacy** of Rome. A legacy is something that is handed down from the past.

Roman architecture has stood the test of time. Architecture is the style in which a building is designed and constructed. Romans used arches, pillars, and domes to build temples, theaters, arenas, and other large, beautiful buildings, some of which still exist today. Many of the building methods and materials the Romans invented—such as concrete—are still used in construction sites around the world.

JANUS—TWO-FACED GOD

Janus was a Roman god with two faces. One face looked back to the past, while the other face looked ahead to the future. Romans worshiped Janus because they understood the importance of studying the past to guide the future.

COMFORTS OF HOME

Romans also invented many of the comforts of modern living. They were the first people to use indoor plumbing, including flush toilets. They invented apartment

Below: The remains of an Ancient Roman toilet with stone seat. People used water and a sponge to clean themselves after using the toilet.

buildings, and central heating systems to warm their homes. They built aqueducts to bring fresh water to the people of Rome, and underground sewers to carry their waste away. They built grand baths to keep people clean and healthy. Romans built a civilized society and filled it with many of the comforts of home we continue to enjoy today.

ROMAN INSTITUTIONS

Romans also created a number of institutions to help keep order in the vast empire. An institution is an official organization that provides structure and rules in a society. Romans developed a legal system that used juries to decide cases fairly. They created a powerful and organized military. Romans also established a fire department, a postal service, and daily newspaper delivery. Rome's institutions helped provide order in society—and continue to do so today.

Below: The Supreme Court in Washington, DC, which was built in classic Ancient Roman style.

Below: The ruins of the Ancient Roman town of Palmyra in Syria. Millions of tourists from all over the world visit Roman sites each year.

WORDS OF WISDOM

There were many great thinkers in Ancient Rome. Vergil and Ovid created incredible poems. Plautus and Terence wrote plays based on Greek comedies. Livy recorded a vast history of the nation. These and other great Romans helped shape and preserve the culture of Rome. Their written works influenced people throughout history, and continue to be studied and admired today.

LATIN ROOTS

Romans wrote and spoke in Latin. Their language became the language of the empire and united people in distant lands. Today, Latin is considered a dead language —that is, one that is no longer used in everyday speech. Latin is still, however, taught in schools and spoken in churches around the world. Latin words are used in science and law. Many modern languages also developed from Latin, including Italian, Spanish, French, Romanian, and Portuguese.

ABCD

Above: A clock face with Roman numerals, and the first four letters of the alphabet in Roman style.

LINK TO TODAY

Romans invented Roman numerals. Roman numerals are a system of letters used to write numbers. For example, the letter V means 5 and the letter X means 10. Roman numerals still appear in writing and on clocks today.

LINK TO TODAY

The English alphabet is based on the Roman, or Latin, alphabet. The Roman alphabet had 23 letters that were written only in capitals. There were no letters J, U, or W in the alphabet. Those letters were added after the fall of the Roman Empire. Although the Roman alphabet changed slightly over time, it formed the foundation of the most widely used alphabet in the world.

Right: An inscription in stone of Ancient Roman text and alphabet. The letter V is now written as U.

ROMAN CALENDAR

The original Roman calendar was invented by Romulus (see pages 6–7). It had 304 days and was divided into 10 months—Martius, Aprilis, Maius, Junius, Quintilis, Sextilis, September, October, November, and December. The second king of Rome added the months January and February—called Januarius and Februarius—and increased the calendar year to 355 days. In 45 B.C.E., Julius Caesar changed the calendar to 365 days. The Julian calendar was used until 1582, when it was changed to the Gregorian calendar used around the world today.

MONTH NAMES

Some months were named for Roman gods and goddesses. January was named for the two-faced god Janus, because it was a time to look back at the year that had passed and look ahead to a new year. March was named after Mars, the god of war, because Romans began fighting wars in spring. June was named for Juno, the goddess of marriage, because Romans considered June the best and luckiest time of year to get married. Other months were named to honor great Roman leaders. July was named for Julius Caesar and August was named for Augustus.

ENGLISH WORDS

Many English words also have roots in Latin. For example, the Latin word for field is *ager* from which we get the English word *agriculture*. The Latin word for book is *liber*. We can find the English word that came from it—and many other words with Latin roots—in a *library*.

Some English words came from Roman mythology. The English word *Herculean* describes something that requires great strength or effort. It comes from the name of the mighty Roman demigod Hercules. The word *mercurial* describes someone who changes their mind or mood suddenly. It comes from the name of the Roman messenger god Mercury, who flew quickly from place to place.

Below: This bronze figure of Mercury is holding a symbol of health.

Below: A silver coin of Augustus Caesar, the first emperor of Rome.

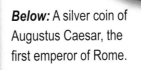

MODERN MYTHOLOGY

Roman myths have influenced and inspired people for thousands of years. Long after the fall of the empire, people continued to share stories about Roman deities. Great writers, such as William Shakespeare, included characters and stories from Roman mythology in their plays. Famous Italian artists, including Michelangelo and Botticelli, portrayed mythical Roman gods in their heavenly paintings and sculptures.

Today, Roman myths continue to play an important part in our culture. We read books

Below: A poster for the film *Gladiator* about life in Ancient Rome.

Left: An illustration of 1882 of three Cupid-like cherubs in the clouds, representing love and happiness.

about great heroes and evil monsters borrowed from Roman mythology. In the *Harry Potter* series, a three-headed dog guards a door to an underground chamber like the Roman underworld. In *The Jungle Book*, Mowgli is cared for by wolves, as were Romulus and Remus. We watch cartoons about a playful pup named Pluto or a strong man named Hercules. We pilot spacecraft called *Apollo*.

ALL AROUND US

Romans believed that the gods and goddesses lived all around them. Today, Roman gods continue to surround us. They live in art, books, and movies that capture our imaginations. They also survive in the history of the empire of Ancient Rome.

RUSSELL CROWE
GLADIATOR

TIME CHART

753 B.C.E. According to Roman mythology, the city of Rome is founded by Romulus after he killed his brother Remus.

509 B.C.E. Romans establish the Roman republic, then the first consuls and senators are chosen

490s B.C.E. The first period of temple building in Rome

451 B.C.E. Romans create the Twelve Tables, their first set of written laws

387 B.C.E. The Gauls sack Rome. To sack is to loot and destroy a captured city

334–264 B.C.E. Roman conquest and colonization of Italy

302–272 B.C.E. The second and main period of temple building

300s–100s B.C.E. Playwrights and poets Plautus, Terence, Livius Andronicus; historian and scholar Cato; and politician Hortensius

200s B.C.E. Greek art and culture brought to Rome

73 B.C.E. Spartacus leads a slave revolt

49 B.C.E. Julius Caesar takes control of Rome.

45 B.C.E. Caesar creates the Julian calendar

44 B.C.E. Caesar is murdered by Roman noblemen

28–19 B.C.E. Vergil writes *The Aeneid*, a poem about the mythical hero Aeneas who became the ancestor of Romans

27 B.C.E. Augustus Caesar becomes the first emperor of Rome, he calls himself "first citizen."

8 C.E. Ovid completes *Metamorphoses*, a 15-book historical poem featuring the gods, goddesses, and myths of Rome

64 C.E. The Great Fire of Rome burns much of the city. According to legend, Emperor Nero sings and plays his lyre—a kind of harp—while the city burns

79 C.E. Mount Vesuvius erupts, covering the cities of Pompeii and Herculaneum in ashes, the Colosseum in Rome is opened.

122–127 C.E. Emperor Hadrian builds a giant stone wall—called Hadrian's Wall—across northern Britain

165–180 C.E. A disease, the plague, sweeps through Rome, killing millions of people

395 C.E. The Roman Empire splits in two—the Western Roman Empire, ruled from Rome, and the Eastern Roman, or Byzantine, Empire, ruled from Constantinople (modern Istanbul)

410 C.E. The Visigoths sack Rome, it is the first time in 800 years that Rome falls to an enemy

476 C.E. The last Western Roman emperor is overthrown

1453 C.E. The Eastern Roman Empire falls

GLOSSARY

ancestor A family member who lived a long time ago

civil war A war fought between people in the same country

courtyard An area enclosed by walls or buildings and open to the air

culture The arts, customs, and ideas of a particular country or a people

deities Gods and goddesses

demigod Someone who is half god and half mortal

divine Like the gods; heavenly

empire A part of the world ruled over by an emperor and contains many previously independent countries

Etruscans Ancient people from a part of Italy, that is now called Tuscany

found To plan and begin the building of a settlement, group, or organization

free All the citizens and non-citizens of Rome who were not slaves

herbs Plants used for food, flavoring, medicine, or perfume

imported Brought in from another country—foreign goods

incense A substance that makes a sweet smell when burned

legacy Something handed down to a successor

mortal A person or being that can die

mortality Life that ends in death

mosaic A picture or design made from small pieces of tile, glass, or stone

myth A very old story, that explains everyday events and often includes gods and other supernatural beings

nymph A beautiful female spirit who lives in rivers, mountains, or other parts of nature

pantheon All the gods, goddesses, and spirits in a religion

pious Describing someone who is very religious

prophecy A prediction of what will happen in the future

relief A carved picture that stands out from its background

shrines Places that contain religious statues or objects and where people worship gods

social ladder A term used to describe the class structure of a society

supernatural Belonging to forces outside of the laws of nature

tapestries Pieces of thick fabric with woven pictures or design often used as wall hangings

tombs Vaults or rooms for burying the dead

underworld The kingdom where Romans believed people went when they died

vain Describing someone who has a very high opinion of himself/herself

virtue A quality that is considered good or desirable in a person

LEARNING MORE

BOOKS

Barber, Nicola. *Ancient Roman Jobs.* New York: PowerKids Press, 2010.

Barber, Nicola. *Ancient Roman Sports and Pastimes.* New York: PowerKids Press, 2010.

Corbishley, Mike. *Ancient Rome* (Cultural Atlas for Young People).
New York: Facts On File, 2003.

Hynson, Colin. *Ancient Rome.* (Historic Civilizations).
Milwaukee: Gareth Stevens Publishing, 2005.

James, Simon. *Ancient Rome.* (Eyewitness Books).
New York: DK Publishing, Inc., 2004.

Macdonald, Fiona. *Romans.* (Hands-On History).
St. Catharines, ON: Crabtree Publishing, 2008.

McCaughrean, Geraldine, and Emma Chichester Clark.
The Orchard Book of Roman Myths. London: Orchard Books, 2003.

Steele, Philip. *Hail! Ancient Romans* (Hail! History).
St. Catharines, ON: Crabtree Publishing, 2011.

Mehta-Jones, Shilpa . *Life in Ancient Rome* (Peoples of the Ancient World).
St. Catharines, ON: Crabtree Publishing, 2005.

WEBSITES

Ancient Rome for Kids
http://rome.mrdonn.org/index.html

BBC Primary History: Romans
www.bbc.co.uk/schools/primaryhistory/romans/

The Roman Empire: Children's Section
www.roman-empire.net/children/index.html

Kidipede—Ancient Rome
http://www.historyforkids.org/learn/romans/index.htm

PBS—The Roman Empire: In the First Century
www.pbs.org/empires/romans/

[Website addresses correct at time of writing—they can change.]

INDEX

Aeneas 4, 39
alphabet 42
animals 4, 18, 20, 21, 30
Apollo 12, 22, 44
aqueducts 6, 39, 40, 41
Aurelius, Marcus 10

baths 28, 29, 41

Caesar, Augustus 10, 38, 39, 43
Caesar, Julius 4, 8, 9, 38, 43
calendar 9, 43
Caligula 10
Ceres 12, 18

Egypt 11
emperor 10, 19, 38, 39, 43
empire 4, 6, 10, 11, 14, 35, 37, 38, 41, 44
Etruscans 6, 40

festivals 12, 25
Forum, the 9, 29, 39

Gaul 7, 8, 34
Gauls 28, 34, 45
geese 28
gladiators 24, 30, 31, 44
Greece 8, 11, 12, 14, 26
Greeks 6, 12, 33, 40, 42, 45

Hadrian 10, 11

Hercules 5, 30, 31, 43, 44
hospitality 5, 19, 35

Isis 11
Italy 6, 8, 23, 24, 26, 39

Juno 4, 12, 13, 21, 26, 27, 28, 39, 43
Jupiter 4, 12, 13, 15, 22, 23, 27, 28, 35, 41

Lares 13
Latin 11, 32, 42, 43

Mars 12, 23, 43
Mercury 12, 13, 23, 27, 35, 43
Minerva 12
Mithras 11
Mount Olympus 14
myth, definition of 4

Narcissus 21
Neptune 12, 22, 33, 39
Nero 10
nymphs 13, 15, 17, 21

Orpheus 17
Ovid 4

Pantheon 12, 15
Pompeii 13, 18, 23, 25

religion 8, 10, 12

Remus 6, 7, 8, 44
republic 7, 8, 9, 36
River Styx 16
Rome, Ancient 4, 6, 10, 15, 18, 19, 20, 29, 30, 32, 42, 44
Romulus 4, 6, 7, 8, 25, 43, 44

Saturn 18, 23
Senate 8, 38
slaves 19, 21, 24, 25, 26, 29, 30
society 24
soldiers 9, 11, 24, 28, 36, 37
Spartacus 24

temples 12, 14, 15, 28, 36, 39, 40

underworld, the 13, 16, 17, 44

Venus 12, 23
Vergil 4, 5, 39, 42
Vesta 12
villas 26, 29
Vulcan 12

wine 18, 19, 24, 34